Written by

Isabella Cooley

Illustrated by

Whimsical Designs by CJ

Description: Includes bibliographical references.

Wesley Chapel, FL: Mommy and Wee Travels, LLC,

Summary: Isabella and her mother travel to Dubai, United Arab Emirates,

learning about the language and culture on the way.

Identifiers: LCCN: 2022919758

ISBN: 979-8-9852287-4-8 (hardcover)

979-8-9852287-5-5 (paperback)

979-8-9852287-3-1 (ebook)

Subjects: LCSH Dubai (United Arab Emirates)–Juvenile literature.

| Dubai (United Arab Emirates)–

Juvenile literature–Description and travel–Juvenile literature.

| Mother and child–Juvenile fiction. |

Travel–Juvenile literature. | BISAC JUVENILE NONFICTION / Travel

| JUVENILE NONFICTION / People & Places /

Classification: LCC DS247.D72 .C66 2023 | DDC 953/.57–dc23

I would like to thank God for always providing us
with tons of love and care. I would like to thank my
godmother and goddad Terolyn and Chad for always
keeping me entertained and helping to take care of me.
I want to thank my god sister Ariel along with my other
god brothers and sisters for being
the best godsiblings ever.

I would like to thank my friends Kaylee and Leon for
being the best friends ever since pre-k. Also, to my
grandparents Mrs. Sandra and Mr. Bo (Robert Sr)
for being the best grandparents ever!

Lastly to my family and fans. Thank you so much for
supporting me and my book series! You guys rock!

Thanks a million

Isabella Cooley

I'm sure that you'll
notice that this is NOT
your everyday travel book.

This book will teach you tons of amazing things
about Dubai! We are going to learn how to say words
in Arabic which is one of the many languages that's
spoken in Dubai. All of our Arabic words that you
will be learning will be in the color red.

BONUS:

At the end of this book, be on the lookout for your Dubai coloring page, word search puzzle, scavenger hunt checklist and fun Dubai workbook page that will teach you many fun facts about this place as well as other fun things to do when visiting.

Marhaba!

I'm Isabella or you can just call me Bella for short! We are going to be camel explorers that's exploring all of Dubai! We are going to have the best camel exploration of our lives!

Come along on this camel ride with me as we learn all of the amazing history of Dubai.

I'm traveling from
New York to Dubai
so this means that
we will be flying
on an airplane for
about 12 hours
nonstop
to Dubai and guess
what, we will
be flying on my
favorite airline
which is **Emirates Airlines**.

I love Emirates Airlines because they always
treat me so special as a big kid. The food is
always fabulous, the tv channels for kids are
never ending and on every flight, kids get an
Emirates adventure kit that's made just for kids!
Oh, also make sure that your parent reserves
your Emirates Airlines kids meal because you
only get a kids meal if one is requested.

We took a **redeye flight** to Dubai! Remember that a redeye flight means that we will fly to Dubai during the night and arrive early in the morning. I try to watch lots of TV on most of the flights, but mommy always falls asleep! Wait! I almost forgot to tell you that you need your passport to fly to Dubai or else they will not let you on the airplane!

*** FUN Fact***

Did you know that in Dubai, the currency (money) has a different name. Money in Dubai is known as "Arab Emirate Dirham" or AED or maybe you can even just say Dirham for short.

Marhaba again! We have landed in Dubai safely! Marhaba means hello in Arabic! In Dubai there are many languages that are spoken but the two most common languages in Dubai are Arabic and English. Dubai is a city that's located in the country of the United Arab Emirates or UAE for short. The airport that we have arrived at is Dubai International Airport (Airport Code- DXB).

Did you know that Dubai was mostly all desert when it was founded in 1833 by the House of Maktoum which is the ruling family of Dubai.

At the airport we will be looking for our fantastic tour guide Mohammad, but we call him Moe for short. Shukran Moe! That's how you say thanks in Arabic. Moe is the best tour guide in Dubai, and I know that because I have been to Dubai three different times and every trip there has been awesome with him!

Since Dubai is so epic, we couldn't just sleep in on our first day. Soooo my mommy and I just took a quick nap then we were off to a meeting and tour of the **Burj Al Arab**. The Burj Al Arab is one of the best resorts in the world and my mom also told me that the Burj Al Arab holds the largest crystal (Swarovski) ceiling in the world as well as other Guiness Book of World Record titles.

After having our meeting and taking our amazing tour of the Burj Al Arab, I had a chance to taste a very different kind of drink. It was 24K Gold Hot Chocolate! My mommy had the 24K Gold Cappuccino that she loved. If you try the hot chocolate, make sure to have your parents add sugar to it because it was disgusting to me without the sugar but once my mom added the sugar to my hot chocolate, it was amazing!

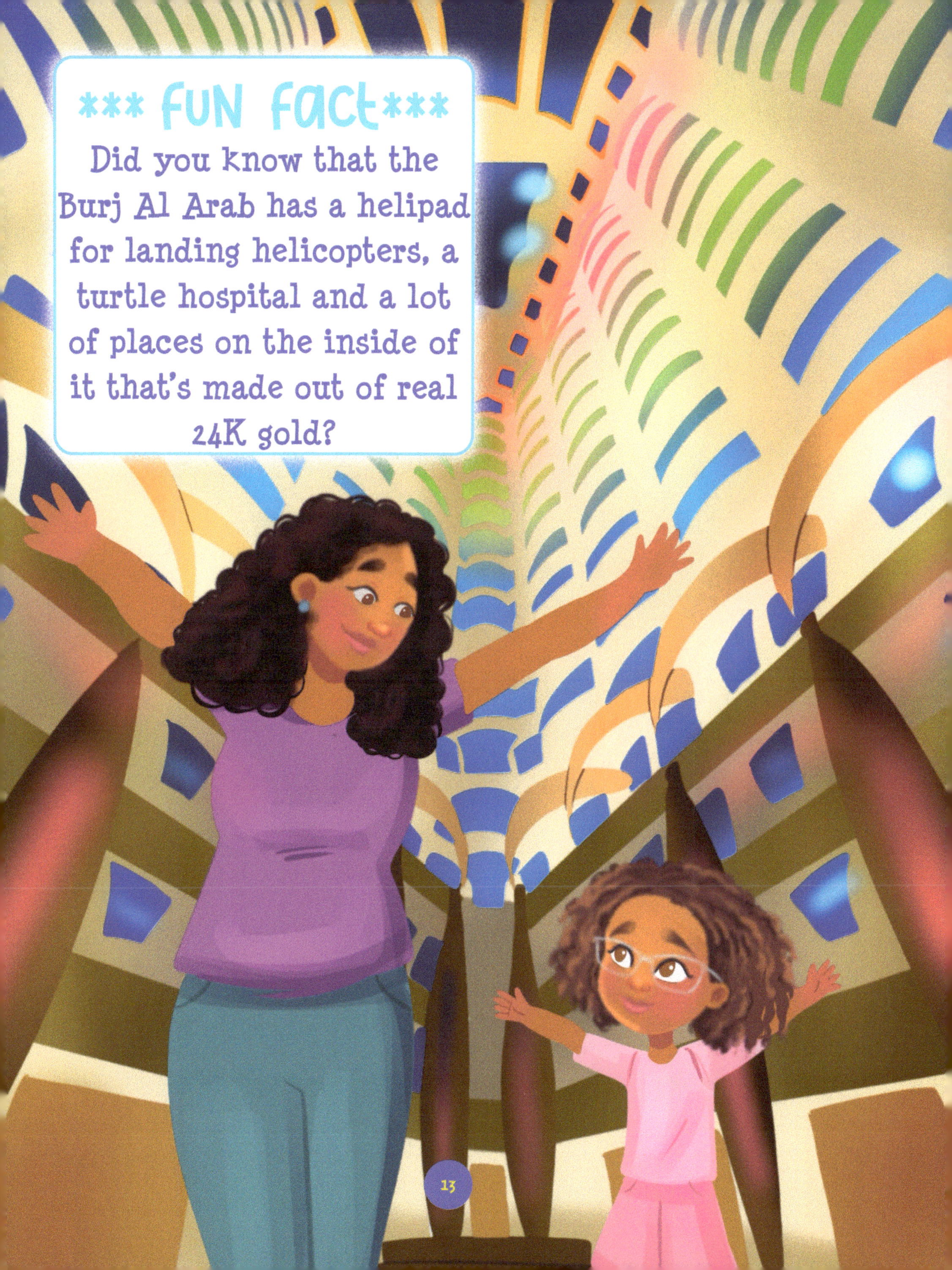

*** FUN FACT ***
Did you know that the Burj Al Arab has a helipad for landing helicopters, a turtle hospital and a lot of places on the inside of it that's made out of real 24K gold?
13

Ohhh have you ever heard of the Burj Khalifa before?

It has one of the fastest elevators in the world plus it's the tallest building in the whole wide world standing at 2,717 feet **Woah!**

This means that over 2.5 Burj Al Arab buildings can stand on top of each other and still NOT be taller than the Burj Khalifa! That's Huge! The Burj Khalifa has some of the prettiest views of Dubai at the *124th floor!!!*

*** FUN FaCt***
The Burj Khalifa elevator can travel
22mph (miles per hour) and reach
the 124th floor in just 1 minute.

Our next stop was to the souks (Arabic market) and gold souks of Dubai. We got to the souks by taking a water taxi down the amazing Dubai Creek. At the souks of Dubai, there are tons of stores to shop for spices, fruits, clothing and a lot of other things like gold!!!

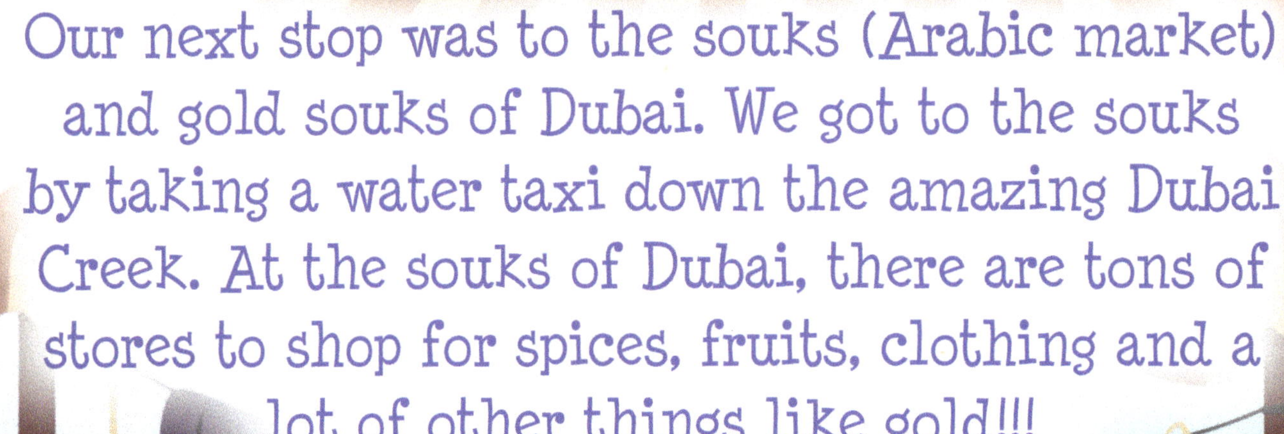

My mommy usually purchases spices and clothing for us to wear at the Sheikh Zayed Grand Mosque (located in Abu Dhabi) while we are at the Dubai souks.

A few of my favorite things to do at the souks of Dubai is to get some delicious camel milk ice cream and to take pictures in front of the Guiness Book of Records largest gold ring in the world!

*** FUN Fact***
The biggest gold ring in the world is called the "Star of Taiba" and it weighs 141 lbs. Thats super duper cool!

On the very next day, our tour guide Moe picked us up for a Dubai day full of fun! On this day, we did a desert safari tour that was complete with an ATV ride, a crazy 4X4 desert car ride, sand duning, an amazing camel ride plus a belly dancing show all with an amazing dinner and a henna tattoo!

My most favorite thing on this tour day was the ATV riding, the sand duning and the belly dancing show. I had tons of fun, but when I was sand duning I fell off of the sand board and my face went straight into the sand. Omg I got sand everywhere!

18

Have you ever been sandboarding or snowboarding before? You must try sandboarding when you come to Dubai. It was so much fun even though I got my face dirty.

This was a crazy fun day!

Do you know that even though Dubai was very hot on our tour day, that I was able to walk on the sand with no shoes WITHOUT burning my feet?

Relaxing is a part of every vacation. On one of our other Dubai vacation days, we chose to relax by jumping on a Dubai City Hop on and Hop Off Bus. While at the very top of the bus, we were able to see so many different things. Lets count to ten in Arabic as we count the big buildings.

*** FUN FACT***

Count To 10 In Arabic With Me
1. wahid (waah-heet)
2. itnan (ihth-naan)
3. talata (theh-lah-theh)
4. arba'a (ahr-uh-bah-ah)
5. hamsa (hahm-sah)
6. sitta (siht-tah)
7. sab'a (sehb-uh ah)
8. tamaniya (theh-mah-nee-yuh)
9. tis'a (tihs-anh)
10. ashra (ahsh-ahr-rah)

Dubai is known for having many world records, but **Abu Dhabi** which is the capital of the United Arab Emirates (UAE) has a world record that is so very pretty to look at. This beauty is known as the **Sheikh Zayed Grand Mosque**. The mosque is known for its white color that's made out of white marble. It is also known for having one of the largest domes and carpets in the world!

One important thing that I remember about our Grand Mosque visit is that it is a very sacred and spiritual place. For our visit, my mommy had to buy special coverings for us. The head covering was called a "hijab" and the dresses were called "abayas".

Have you ever heard of Atlantis? Well guess what? There is a huge Atlantis in Dubai as well!

I've been to a few Atlantis resorts, but this Dubai Atlantis has a waterpark named Aquaventure Waterpark and it is one of my favorite waterparks. My favorite favorite ride at this waterpark is the Aquaconda Slide. On this slide we got into a water raft, then our raft was let go into this huge water slide. Let's Go *Weeeeeeeeeeeeeeee!!!* At the end of this slide, there is a huge water splash as we landed into the pool that's at the end of this slide. We always get super wet when on this slide!

Another thing that I really like about the Dubai Atlantis is the **Lost Chambers Aquarium**. It's always super cool at the aquarium and lunch is always yummy at Atlantis. If you love aquariums like I do, another epic Dubai aquarium to check out is the **Dubai Mall Aquarium**. This aquarium is gigantic, and it even has an underground tunnel that's located under a tank that has sharks and rays in it. This means epic shark pictures! I love aquariums so much and I want to know all about your next aquarium visit!

*** FUN FACT ***

The aquarium and lagoon at Atlantis Dubai is home to over 250 different species of fish as well as 65,000 other marine animals. How cool!

A trip to Dubai is never complete without tasting some of the local Arabic foods. For me, I really like the chicken that's there in Dubai. The chicken wraps are the best if you ask me. So, I would say that my favorite favorite Arabic food is the chicken.

IT'S THE BEST!!! I remember when we were visiting, my mommy made me try a **falafel** sandwich with some **hummus** on the side. I thought that it was going to be disgusting but guess what? It was DELICIOUS!!!

So don't be afraid to try new foods like camel milk ice cream and other things while traveling.

There's so many amazing thing to do in Dubai that it can't be done in one visit unless you stay on vacation there for a very very long time. Thank you soooo much for coming on this Dubai exploration with us and I can't wait for you to come back to Dubai with me.

Remember if you have extra time in Dubai, you should also checkout our checklist of must do activities in Dubai.

Ohhhhhh we can't wait to see all of your Dubai vacation pictures. Don't forget to have your parents tag us on your next vacation pictures so that we can explore the world together or maybe we can meet up for a group trip someday. This would be awesome!

Tag Us On Your Next Journey
#ExplorerOfMommyAndWeeTravels

BONUS

Camel explores don't forget to use your Dubai coloring page and word search puzzle on your next journey. Also, whenever you come to Dubai, your scavenger hunt checklist will help you to uncover some other hidden fun places to explore!

- ☐ Atlantis Dubai
- ☐ Burj Al Arab
- ☐ Burj Khalifa
- ☐ Dubai Aquarium & Underwater Zoo
- ☐ Dubai Frame
- ☐ Dubai Miracle Garden
- ☐ Global Village
- ☐ Glow Park Dubai
- ☐ Kite Beach or La Mer Beach
- ☐ Ski Dubai
- ☐ The Dubai Fountain
- ☐ The Dubai Mall
- ☐ The Dubai Museum Of The Future
- ☐ Water Taxi Ride On The Dubai Creek
- ☐ Wild Wadi Waterpark

Thanks For
Exploring
Dubai
With Me

Lets Explore Dubai With Isabella Workbook

```
        W B T G U S R B
      S A Q L T A T Y R Z Q L
      N U K L Z B T B B K X Q U U
    H V S Q V L G G L U J N C E I D
  Z Y W I W E D E V K X D G R G H E W
  M K K T M M U D B W U A H S N C V W
F O Z K N B A B O I A V A V A K E F Y A
C B H D A N R A S A I S P T C B U F F A
Q A R Q L W F I A B S D I N Y Q I O C D
Z B M T T P I C C U P S Y C T D X U S N
W N A E A W A R V D J E R T A J B D N Q
X T D R L B B E M E Z G H L L X E J Q R
P U H A A P U E B U R J K H A L I F A A
R U S B Q L D K J M O S Q U E L W X B E
  M O D R I A F T R E S E D F N L A N
  T O E X H Z J X Q J B Z D I R H A M
    D X J I T N R Y B O A B B A E Z
      Y S G K F X U F P Y G R B W
      A P P Q L Q B M R A Z C
        A J V W Z D M Y
```

WORD LIST:

ABU DHABI	CAMEL	DUBAI CREEK	MOSQUE
ATLANTIS	DESERT	DUBAI FRAME	SOUKS
BURJ AL ARAB	DIRHAM	ISABELLA	
BURJ KHALIFA	DUBAI	MARAHABA	

Name ______________________________

Lets Explore Dubai With Isabella Workbook

1. What two languages are spoken in Dubai? ________ & _________ .

2. How do you say "hello" in Arabic _______ ?

3. What was Isabella's favorite food to eat in Dubai? _______________

4. What country is Dubai in? _________

5. What is the capital of United Arab Emirates? ____________

6. How do you say "thank you" in Arabic? __________

7. What is the tallest building in the world? _____________

8. How do you say " seven" in Arabic? ________

9. What is the headwrap that many women wear in the United Arab Emirates? _________

10. What's the name of the currency (money) that's used in Dubai? _________